No Longer I

Sharing Christ's Gospel Narrative

Dennis J. Billy, C.Ss.R.

En Route Books and Media, LLC
Saint Louis, MO

⊕*ENROUTE*
Make the time

En Route Books and Media, LLC

5705 Rhodes Avenue

St. Louis, MO 63109

contact@enroutebooksandmedia.com

Cover Credit: Sebastian Mahfood

ISBN-13: 978-1-956715-79-8

LCCN: 2022943304

In fond memory of
Rev. Arthur Gildea, C.Ss.R.
"Artie"
"The Wrench"
(1942-2022)

I have been crucified with Christ;
And it is no longer I who live,
But it is Christ who lives in me
Gal 2:19-20

Table of Contents

Introduction 1

Ch. One: Christ's Gospel Narrative 3

Ch. Two: Interpreting Christ's Gospel
  Narrative 25

Ch. Three: Embracing Christ's Gospel
  Narrative 47

Ch.Four: Living Christ's Gospel Narrative 67

Ch. Five: Sharing Christ's Gospel Narrative 87

Conclusion 107

Introduction

Christ entered our world and gave himself completely to us to the point of dying for us, to become nourishment for us and a source of hope. This single sentence embraces every element of what I call Christ's Gospel narrative. It embraces the central mysteries of the Catholic faith: Christ's Incarnation, his Passion and Death, his sacrificial meal known as the Eucharist, and his Resurrection and Ascension into heaven. This book examines this narrative through five different lenses. Chapter One, "Christ's Gospel Narrative," looks at the narrative itself, each of its four movements, and the mysteries they reveal. Chapter Two, "Interpreting Christ's Gospel Narrative," explores at the various ways the narrative has been interpreted and argues for the importance of maintaining a continuity between the Jesus of History and the Christ of Faith. Chapter Three, "Embracing Christ's Gospel Narrative," focuses on the importance of ongoing conversion in the Christian life and how the threefold movement of purgation, illumination, and union moves us further along the way of holiness. Chapter Four, "Living Christ's Gospel Narrative," considers how our spiritual journey unfolds within the wounded world we live in and offers some suggestions about how we can remain firm in our faith, vibrant in our hope, and selfless in our love for others. Chapter Five, "Sharing Christ's Gospel Narrative," views Jesus' public ministry as a way of understanding how the Church should share the Gospel message and offers some practical suggestions for doing so. Each chapter concludes with a series of reflection questions to help the reader probe more deeply into the meaning of Christ's Gospel narrative and a prayer that asks Jesus to send his Spirit to dwell within our hearts and make his abode there. A conclusion summarizes the main points of the book and encourages the reader to make the Christ narrative his or her own. Those who do will have a transforming effect on those they encounter and understand what the Apostle Paul meant when he said, "[I]t is no longer I who live, but it is Christ who lives in me" (Gal 2:20).[1]

---

[1] All Scripture quotations come from *Holy Bible: New Revised Standard Version with Apocrypha* (New York: Oxford University Press, 1989).

Chapter One

Christ's Gospel Narrative

"If any want to become my followers, let them deny themselves and take up their cross daily and follow me" (Lk 9:29). These words of Jesus reveal the true challenge of Christian discipleship. To follow Jesus means that we must decide each day to pick up the cross he has asked us to carry and walk in his footsteps. He asks us to make his narrative our own, so that he can make our narrative his. The beauty of Christian discipleship is that Jesus wishes to have intimate friendship with each of us: "I do not call you servants any longer, because the servant does not know what the master is doing; but I have called you friends, because I have made known to you everything that I have heard from my Father." (Jn 15:15). Jesus wishes to share with us the same intimate knowledge of the Father that he has shared with his earliest disciples. This can happen, however, only if we accompany him on his journey and have a clear idea of just what that journey entails.

In this chapter, I will offer you what I believe is the underlying Gospel narrative of Jesus' redemptive journey and show how it should resonate in the life of anyone who wishes to be called his disciple. I will do so by developing a four-fold movement which elsewhere I have termed the Christ kernel, or the fundamental principle of Christology: (1) He entered our world in the mystery of the Incarnation, (2) gave himself to us completely in his public ministry and in the mystery of his Passion and Death, (3) became nourishment for us in the mystery of the Eucharist, and (4) a source of hope for us in the mysteries of his Resurrection and Ascension into heaven. Anyone who wishes to be one of Jesus' disciples must embrace in his or her own life these four basic movements of this basic Gospel narrative. Because each of us is unique and has a particular role to play in God's providential plan, this narrative will unfold in your life and my life in different ways. Every relationship with Christ is unique and irreplaceable. He wishes us to dwell in his heart so that he can dwell in ours. Let us examine each of the movements of Christ's Gospel narrative in more detail.

He Entered Our World

When talking with many non-Christians of the secular Western world who stand outside the Judeo-Christian tradition, I have found that one of the main difficulties they have in accepting Christianity is that they find the idea of God's entering our world and becoming human simply untenable. How can the infinite mix with the finite? How can the realm of spirit enter that of the material? How could it possibly do so? And why? They have a hard time wrapping their minds around the idea that God, who is Spirit, would want to have anything to do with the world of matter? Their idea of God (if they have one at all) is that of an impersonal, detached, transcendent force outside the bounds of physical reality. This force may keep the world in existence, but that is about it. For better or worse, the universe has pretty much been left on its own and must fend for itself. The idea of this divine force manifesting itself in the here-and-now to them seems outlandish, even childish. It belittles the very notion of God to say that he has the capacity to step into the boundaries of time and space and mingle, let alone walk the earth as a man in some marginal Jewish settlement some 2,000 years ago. They view Christianity as a myth embraced by simple (even primitive) minds. The Christian God, for them, is a projection onto the spiritual world of humanity's deepest hopes and yearnings. For them, man was not made in the image and likeness of God, but vice versa. God was created in the image and likeness of man.

In the words of J. B. Phillips, my response to such thoughts is, "Your God is too small."[2] Members of the Western secular world either do not believe in God or have such a confined (and narrow) understanding of who or what God is, or simply don't believe in God's existence altogether. "To believe in God is irrational," they say. Since his existence cannot be proven empirically, they conclude that he must not exist at all. They claim that their empirical understanding of scientific knowledge is the only valid instrument for determining what is true and what is not. How sad. The scientific

---

[2] J. B. Phillips, *Your God Is too Small* (New York: Macmillan, 1961).

method arose out of a Western culture imbued with faith. It was developed by Christians and was ultimately used to undermine the fundamental claims of the Gospel Message. As Pope Emeritus Benedict XVI points out, the Church accepts science, but it rejects the ideological premises of scientism, which holds that scientific knowledge is the only lens through which humanity should interpret reality. Scientism, he goes on to say, has lost sight of the boundaries within which it could properly operate. By overreaching its grasp, it does harm to the human enterprise which, at least within the Catholic tradition, rests first and foremost on the call to Happiness.[3] Catholicism is not suspicious of reason but holds that *fides et ratio* ("faith and reason") complement one another and that faith even enlightens reason, which has been darkened because of our original fall from grace.[4] The proponents of scientism ultimately conclude that God

---

[3] See, for example Benedict XVI's encyclical, *Spe salvi,* nos. 16-31.

[4] See, for example John Paul II's encyclical, *Fides et ratio*, nos. 36-48.

either does not exist or is irrelevant to today's world. I beg to differ.

Christians believe that God created the world and that with him all things are possible. We believe that man was created in God's image and likeness and that, as such, he can have an intimate friendship with his Creator. God, in turn, also wishes to have an intimate friendship with us and, to do so, has it in his power to enter our world, become one of us, and walk beside us. He did so to experience his creation from the inside looking out, to heal a world wounded by sin, transform it, and do so in such a way that our friendship with him would be possible. Friendship with God, we might say, represents the height of his threefold action. In it, the creative activity of the Father, the redemptive action of the Son, and the sanctifying action of the Spirit converge. God, in other words, entered the world he created to redeem it and sanctify it, so that we might be capable of sharing in his divine life. In the words of Athanasius of Alexandria, "God became man so that man might become divine."[5]

---

[5] *On the Incarnation*, 54.3.

Christians, in other words, believe that just as man is *capax Dei* ("capable of God") so too is God *capax hominis* ("capable of man"). That is to say, the all-powerful God, Creator of the universe, is and could write himself into the very pattern of his own creation. Not only did he leave vestiges of himself in every part of his creation and create man in his image and likeness, but he also decided to enter the world himself, walk the earth, and dwell among us to elevate us, transform us, and divinize us. Jesus Christ, the New Adam, is the firstborn of the new creation. In becoming man, he was like us in all things but sin (Heb 4:15). He came to give us life and a share in his own divinity.

He Gave Himself Completely

Jesus, however, did not merely enter our world. The kenotic self-emptying of his divinity into our humanity continued throughout his earthly life (1) in his hidden life at Nazareth, (2) in his public ministry in Galilee, Samaria, and Judea, and (3) in his suffering and death in Jerusalem on the hill of Golgotha. This second movement of

Jesus' Gospel narrative thus contains three phases. Let us examine each of them, one by one, as he himself experienced them.

Jesus' Hidden Life. Although he was born in Bethlehem in Judea, Jesus was raised in the town of Nazareth in the hill country of Galilee. He spent most of his life there, attended synagogue, learned the Torah, and took up his foster father's trade as a carpenter. Before his public ministry, he spent a good thirty years giving himself to his family and kinfolk, to his artisan's trade, and to his Jewish faith. His thorough knowledge of the Law and the Prophets goes well beyond what other men of his time would have acquired and indicates that he spent hours listening to the texts read aloud at synagogue and reading them whenever the opportunity arose. When he visited Jerusalem with his parents at the age of twelve, he visited the Temple and astonished the teachers there with the depth of his wisdom (Lk 2:41-52). Both human and divine, this wisdom came from his intimate relationship with his Father in heaven and from the earnestness with which he applied himself to learning the various laws and customs of the Jewish faith. The devotion of his parents, Mary and Joseph, surely encouraged him in this. They knew their son was specially chosen by God yet did not completely understand the nature of his call. As Jesus asked them, "Why were you searching for me? Did you not know that I must be in my Father's house? (Lk 2:49). Jesus' hidden life was a period of preparation for events still to come. During this time, he "grew in and became strong, filled with wisdom; and the favor of God was upon him" (Lk 2:40).

Jesus' Public Ministry. Jesus' public ministry begins with his baptism in the Jordan by John the Baptist. As the Gospel of Mark describes it, "And just as he was coming up out of the water, he saw the heavens torn apart and the Spirit descending like a dove. And a voice came from heaven, 'You are my Son, the Beloved; with you I am well pleased'"(Mk 1:10-11). The Spirit then drives him out into the wilderness for forty days to live with the wild beasts and to be tempted by the Evil One with promises of pleasure, power, and possessions. Jesus then gathers a group of disciples and goes about preaching the coming of God's Kingdom, saying that it is coming yet already in their midst.

As his Sermon on the Mount (Mt 5-7) and such parables as "The Good Samaritan" (Lk 10:25-37) and "The Prodigal Son" (Lk 15:1-32) reveal, he preaches a message of mercy, love, and forgiveness. As seen in his cure of the paralytic in Capernaum (Mk 2:1-12), he even goes so far as to forgive the sins of those who come to him for healing. Doing so puts him at odds with the Scribes and Pharisees, who view such actions as forgiving someone's sins and healing on the Sabbath as blasphemous. As his reputation as a preacher and a healer grows, Jesus amasses a large following. Large crowds follow him in the hope of being healed of their spiritual and/or physical wounds. He casts out demons (Mk 1:21-28), cures lepers (Mk 1:40-45), heals a paralytic (Mk 2:1-12), heals a man with a withered hand (Mk 1:3:1-6), turns water into wine (Jn 2:1-12), feeds multitudes (Mt 14:13-21, walks on water (Mt 14:22-3), even brings the dead back to life (Jn 11:1-44). Jesus public ministry culminates in his triumphant entrance to Jerusalem and ultimately leads to his death by crucifixion.

Jesus' Passion and Death. Jesus and his disciples eventually make their way to Jerusalem, the place where he knows he will be unjustly tried and sentenced to a most horrible death. The night before he dies, he celebrates a parting meal with his apostles, washes their feet, and afterwards brings them to the Garden of Gethsemane, at the foot of the Mount of Olives. While there, he goes off to pray and agonizes over what is about to happen to him. In the midst of this intense inner pain and suffering, he sweats droplets of blood and asks the Father to take the cup of suffering away from him. Still, he is intent on doing the Father's will rather than his own (Lk 22:43). The events leading to his death follow in rapid succession.[6] Although the particulars of Jesus' passion differ in the synoptic gospels and in the gospel of John, a synthetic presentation would look something like this. Jesus is betrayed by Judas (Mt 26:20-25), arrested by the chief priests and captains of the Temple guard (Mt 26:47-56), brought before the Sanhedrin (Mt 26: 57-56), sent to Pilate (Mt 27:1-2), who then sends him to Herod

---

[6] The passion narratives appear in Mt 26-28, Mk 14-16, Lk 22-24, and Jn 18-21.

(Lk 23:6-12), who sends him back to the Roman Procurator (Lk 23:13-25). Pilate then has him scourged, during which time he is mocked by the Roman soldiers, who put a crown of thorns on his head and dress him in a purple robe (Mt 27:27-31: Lk 23:15). Pilate finds no case against him and wants to release him, but he gives in to the pressure of the chief priests and temple guards who want him crucified (Lk 23:20-25; Jn 19:12-16). Wishing to avoid an incident, he sends Jesus off to be crucified on the hill of Golgotha just outside the walls of the city (Jn 19:17-22). Jesus is made to carry his cross along what is now called the *Via Dolorosa* to the top of Golgotha. Along the way, he stumbles and falls. The soldiers enlist Simon of Cyrene to carry the cross part of the way (Mt 27:1). There he is nailed to a cross, which is raised between two thieves (Lk 23:33-34, 39-43). Nearly all his disciples deserted him: Judas betrayed him; Peter denied him three times (Mt 26:69-75); the others dispersed in fear and went into hiding. Only Mary, his mother, Mary, the wife of Clopas, Mary Magdalen, and John, the beloved disciple, remained with him to the end. Jesus' passion and death represents his ultimate gift of self (Jn 19:25-27). He embraces death itself to free humanity from the slavery of sin and its bondage to the Evil One. His passion and death were historical events that also transcended the finite boundaries of time and space.

He Became Nourishment for Us

This second movement of Jesus' Gospel narrative, which encompasses his hidden life, public ministry, and suffering and death on the cross, leads to the third, whereby he becomes nourishment for us in the Eucharist. The night before he died, Jesus had a final meal with his disciples. At this Last Supper, he took bread, blessed it, broke it, and passed it around to his disciples saying it was his Body which would be given up for them. Then his took a cup of wine, again said the blessing, and passed it around to his disciples saying it was his Blood, the Blood of the New and Eternal Covenant. He then asked his disciples to celebrate this breaking of the bread and the passing of the cup of wine in his memory.

Jesus' Last Supper with his disciples was the first Christian Eucharist. It foreshadowed and culminated in his sacrifice on Golgotha the following day when he uttered the words, "It is finished" (Jn 19:30). In the transformation of mere bread and wine into his Body and Blood, it pointed to his Glorified and Risen Presence on Easter morning. By asking us to eat and drink of his Body and Blood, it reminds us that he himself is the "Bread of Life" (Jn 6:35) and that "…unless you eat of the flesh of the Son of Man and drink of his blood, you have no life in you" (Jn 6:53). Jesus, in other words, not only entered our world and gave himself to us completely, to the point of laying down his life for us, but also became food and nourishment for us. Whenever we receive the Eucharist, we eat and drink a heavenly food, one that will divinize us over time and conform us more and more unto the person of Christ, so much so that we will be able to say with the Apostle Paul, "…it is no longer I who live, but it is Christ who lives in me" (Gal 2:20). If we become members of Christ's Body through Baptism, it is through the Eucharist that we are given the nourishment and strength to make our way in our pilgrim journey through this life and travel into the mystery of God in the life to come.

When we eat simple bread and drink common wine, our body's digestive system breaks them down and absorbs the nutrients contained therein in such a way that they become a part of our own flesh and blood. Whenever we receive the Body and Blood of our Lord Jesus in the Eucharist, however, the reverse process happens. Rather than making the consecrated bread and wine a part of ourselves, they consume us and incorporate us more deeply into the Christ's glorified existence. This manna from heaven, in other words, absorbs us into the Christ's divinized humanity, unites us with his divinity, and allows us to enter the presence of the Father. His Spirit flows through our veins and unites us to him in much the same way that the body is united to the soul and the soul to the spirit. No one knows just how this happens, but then again, few of us understand the intricacies of human digestion yet still we eat and drink to stay alive. Christ has given us his own flesh and blood to eat and drink so that we might share in his divine life and have it in abundance.

Jesus loves us so much that he wants to become the very food and drink that will lead us to God and enable to share in his divine friendship. "Paradise for God," it is said, "is the heart of man."[7] The Eucharist is the way God befriends us so that he might dwell in our hearts, and we might dwell in his. Each time we celebrate the Eucharist, the Lord Jesus celebrates his Last Supper with his closest friends and most intimate companions. The Eucharist is a sacrificial meal that brings Jesus into our midst in a variety of ways. He is present in the person of the priest, in the proclamation of the Word, in the consecrated bread and wine, and in the worshiping community, the community of saints who ever since the early days of the Church were known as the "friends of God."

He Became a Source of Hope for Us

The fourth and final movement of Jesus' Gospel narrative is his resurrection from the dead. The

---

[7] Alphonsus de Liguori, *The Way to Converse Always and Familiarly with God*, 1.

Apostle Paul offers one of the earliest written versions of Jesus' resurrection appearances: "For I handed on to you as of first importance what I in turn had received: that Christ died for our sins in accordance with the scriptures, and that he was buried, and that he was raised on the third day in accordance with the scriptures, and that he appeared to Cephas, then to the twelve. Then he appeared to more than five hundred brothers and sisters at one time, most of whom are still alive, though some have died. Then he appeared to James, then to all the apostles. Last of all, as to one untimely born, he appeared to me" (1 Cor 15:3-8).

The Gospel accounts have him appearing also to Mary Magdalen (Mk 16:9; Jn 20:1-18), to Mary and the other Mary as they were returning from the sepulcher (Mt 28:9-10), to Peter (Lk 24:34), to two disciples on the road to Emmaus (Mk 16:12; Lk 24:13-31), to all the apostles except for Thomas (Mk 16:14; Jn 20:19-25), to all the apostles with Thomas (Jn 20:26-29), to some of disciples as they were fishing on the sea of Galilee (Jn 21:1-13), to some disciples on a mountain in Galilee (Mt 28:16-18), to the apostles and others during the forty days prior to his ascension (Acts 1:2-3), and at the time of his ascension to heaven (Lk 24:50-51; Acts 1:6-12). These appearances affirm that Jesus was raised bodily from the dead but in a transfigured, glorified form. The accounts attest to Jesus's bodily resurrection, that he was not a phantom or a ghost, but that his body was raised from the dead and that he ate and drank with his disciples, and that he even showed them the wounds in his hands, feet, and side.

Jesus' resurrection kindles in us the hope that we too will one day rise from the dead. He died and rose so that we might die and rise with him. The Gospel narrative is intimately tied to the objective fact of Jesus' resurrection from the dead. As the Apostle Paul states, "If there is no resurrection of the dead, then Christ has not been raised; and if Christ has not been raised, then our proclamation has been in vain and your faith has been in vain. We are even found to be misrepresenting God, because we testified of God that he raised Christ— whom he did not raise if it is true that the dead are not raised. For if the dead are not raised, then Christ has not been raised. If Christ has not been raised , your faith is futile, and you are still in your sins" (1 Cor 15: 13-17). But if Jesus was, in fact, raised from the dead, then our faith is well founded, and we have everything to hope and look forward to. What is more, Jesus' mother, Mary, is yet another reason for us to hope that we too will one day rise from death.

According to tradition, after his resurrection, Jesus appeared first to his mother, Mary, before anyone else. Although the Gospels do not refer to this appearance to Mary, it is argued that it would be fitting for him to do so. According to the dogma of the Assumption, at the end of her earthly sojourn, Mary's body and soul were taken up (assumed) into heaven to share in the fullness of the resurrected life made possible by her Son's paschal mystery. As such, she was the first human being to experience the fullness of the redemption. Every other saint in heaven is awaiting the resurrection of their bodies at the end of time. Because of her unique role in God's providential plan for humanity's redemption, Mary was given the privilege to be the first to experience the first fruits of the redemptive action of her Son. She has now what we hope one day hope to have. That is why we call her "our life, our sweetness, and our hope." Jesus' resurrection from the dead and Mary's living the resurrected life in her glorified body at the right hand of her Son deepens out hope that we too may one day share in this resurrected and glorified existence.

Conclusion

What can we say by way of conclusion? The underlying Gospel narrative says that God entered our world in the person of Jesus Christ, gave himself to us completely to the point of dying for us, became nourishment for us in the sacrament of the Eucharist, and a source of hope for us by virtue of his resurrection from the dead and ascension into heaven. Because of him, his mother Mary shares in her Son's transfigured, glorified existence, the fullness of her Son's redemptive action. Like her, we hope one day to have a share in her Son's risen life.

Christ's Gospel narrative is another way of talking about the four mysteries of his Incarnation, his Passion and Death, his presence in the Eucharist, and his Resurrection and Ascension. The fourfold movement of this narrative underlies the entire Christian message and seeks to root itself in the life of every believer. Christ's story, in other words, is also our own. The closer we come to him, the more will his redemptive narrative be deeply engrained in the fabric of our lives. Christ will dwell in our hearts and live out his Gospel narrative in us. He will live in our hearts, and we will live in his.

We will then find ourselves entering the worlds of others, giving ourselves to them completely, becoming nourishment and a source of hope for them. Christ's Gospel narrative will shine through us and lead others to him. They, in turn, will reach out to others, and the kingdom of God will continue to spread from heart to heart. God's kingdom, in other words, is already here, both within our hearts and in our midst and will continue to grow as Christ's Gospel narrative finds its way into every human heart to shed the light of God's compassionate love and mercy into those corners that have been darkened by the deceptive allurements of egoism and sin.

Christ's Gospel Narrative

- What is unique about Christ's Gospel narrative?
- How would you characterize it?
- Did you find it easy to understand?
- Did you find it difficult to fathom?
- If asked, would you be able to explain to someone else?

Prayer

Lord, help me to make your story my own. Live in me so that I may live in you.

Chapter Two

Interpreting Christ's Gospel Narrative

The four-fold movement underlying Christ's Gospel narrative needs not only to be told, again and again throughout the corridors of time, but also interpreted and personally appropriated by those who encounter it. It needs to be told in such a way that it connects with people living in different countries, cultures, and historical epochs, so that they can find relevant meaning in it for their lives. Such interpretations must be in continuity with Christ's Gospel narrative itself but told (and retold) in such a way that it resonates in the hearts of those who hear it. In this chapter, we will propose a way to do this that is faithful to the narrative itself yet offers insights into how the reader or listener can find deeply personal meaning in it for their lives. We will show how Christ's Gospel narrative can be read in such a way that it preserves the continuity between the Jesus of History and the Christ of Faith, as well as enables those who encounter it to discover in Christ's Gospel narrative profound spiritual meaning for their lives.

The Jesus of History and the Christ of Faith

When the Scriptures were first being examined through the eyes of the historical-critical method in the late-seventeenth and early eighteenth centuries, the interpretive approach seeking to explain them through the lens of its historical setting (or *sitz im leben*, as it is called in German), some biblical scholars introduced the distinction between what they called the Jesus of History and the Christ of Faith. Influenced by the overt rationalism of the Enlightenment, their thinking was that, although Biblical accounts were rooted in history, they also were heavily affected by myth and faith-based imagination.

One of the assumptions of this approach was that miracles do not exist and that the presence of them in the Biblical narratives were purely symbolic and without any historical grounding. As far as the Gospels were concerned, Jesus' miracles were a reading back into history of Jesus' day convictions that belonged to the early Christian communities. As a result, they posited a fundamental discontinuity between the two. The historical Jesus was considered a great Jewish prophet and teacher, but not someone who could walk on water, calm the sea, or feed the multitudes through the multiplication of the loaves and fishes. These, they surmised, were later accretions added by the early Christian writers to underscore their conviction that Jesus was divine and did, in fact, rise from the dead.

As the historical-critical method became the dominant lens for interpreting the Scriptures (especially among Protestant scholars), the divide between the Jesus of History and the Christ of Faith grew larger and larger, so much so that many of them saw an utter disconnect between the two. In the twentieth century, the German biblical scholar Rudolf Bultmann (1884-1976) simply accepted this distinction and ultimately declared that any attempt to discover the historical Jesus was irrelevant because the Gospel narratives were too heavily influenced by Christian myth. He then attempted a "demythologization" of the Gospel narrative which sought to uncover the existential meaning of the Gospels that would speak to the heart of his contemporaries.[8] Although his influence on Biblical criticism has waned in recent decades and the distinction between the Jesus of History and the Christ of Faith is now seen as more continuous (or at least porous), the debate on the relationship between the two continues to this day. Catholic biblical scholars, who were encouraged by Pope Pius XII in his encyclical *Divino Afflante Spiritu* (1943) to employ the historical-critical method as a way of placing the Gospels in their historical context and discover their literal and historical meaning, tend to see a fundamental continuity between the two. They do so because they affirm that Jesus did rise from the dead and, after his ascension to heaven, continued to live in the community of believers, his Body the Church, through his Spirit who descended on them at Pentecost and continues to do so to this day.

---

[8] See Rudolf Bultmann, "New Testament and Mythology," in *Kerygma and Myth: A Theology Debate*, ed. Hans Werner Bartsch, trans. Reginald H. Fuller (New York: Harper & Row, 1941), 1-44.

Myth Became Fact

An alternative way of looking at the relationship between myth and the Gospel narrative, one promoted by many prominent traditional Christians, is what may be termed "myth-fulfillment." This approach sees a fundamental continuity between the historical Jesus and the Christ of Faith. The latter, in this line of thinking, is one with the Jesus of History. According to this perspective, Jesus really *did* rise from the dead! His rising, however, was not a mere resuscitation, as in the case of the raising of Lazarus (Jn 11:1-44), but an actual transformation of his historical existence to a glorified form. When seen in this light, the Jesus of History—his body and blood, soul, and divinity—was lifted-up into a transcendent dimension of existence, while all the while maintaining its connection with historical time and space. This glorified existence was, at one and the same time, both spiritual and material. The spiritual and material realms, in other words, were lifted-up, transformed, and empowered to exist in a dimension beyond those of time and space.

Probably the most eloquent proponent of this point of view is C. S. Lewis (1898-1963), a tutor of medieval and renaissance literature for most of his adult life at Magdalene College, Oxford, and in the last years of his life as a professor at Magdalene College, Cambridge, who also was one of the great Christian apologists of the twentieth century.[9] Lewis was born and raised in the Anglican communion but became an atheist at the age of fifteen. He returned to Christianity through the influence of two of his friends at Oxford, J. R.R. Tolkien and Hugo Dyson. Lewis's main difficulty with Christianity was that he viewed it as just another mythological expression of the dying and rising god that existed in many of the pagan mythologies of the ancient world that were typically associated with fertility rites, the changing of the seasons, and the autumn harvest. Lewis thought along the lines of James Frazier's *The Gold Bough*, a late-nineteenth century work in comparative theology that brought

---

[9] See C. S. Lewis, "Myth Became Fact," in *God in the Dock: Essays on Theology and Ethics* (Grand Rapids, MI: William B. Eerdmans Publishing Company, 1970), 63-67.

out many parallels between the dying and rising of Jesus and such ancient pagan deities as Osiris, Adonis, and Attis. Tolkien and Dyson convinced Lewis that these early pagan myths were merely a foreshadowing of the Gospel narrative. They were a sort of natural revelation that pointed to the coming of Jesus of Nazareth, who was the one true dying and rising God, the Myth that had become Fact.

This "myth-fulfillment" approach to Christ's Gospel narrative denies that the Gospel is fundamentally a myth in need of being demythologized before it can have any relevant meaning for today's world. It represents, instead, the fulfillment of the hopes and dreams of the entire ancient world by saying that God prepared for the reception of the one true myth by leaving vestiges of that myth in the imagination and memory of the pagan world. When seen in this light, the Gospel represents the myth par excellence that has entered our world and become historical fact in the dying and rising of the historical Jesus who by his death and resurrection also became the Christ of faith. His dying and rising, however, is not a matter of being in sync with human fertility and the changing of the seasons, but of our own death and hope that we will continue to exist after it. "God became man so that man might become divine," as St. Athanasius tells us. God, who is capable of man (*capax hominis*) entered our world and became one of us. Christ's Gospel narrative represents the fulfillment of the myth of the dying and rising god of the ancient world. The "myth-fulfillment" understanding of the Gospels, the exact opposite of Bultmann's "demythologizing" approach. The Jesus of History is one and the same with the Christ of Faith: one Person who has existed in history and who now lives a glorified existence beyond the boundaries of space and time.

The Senses of Scripture

Questions arise: How are we to interpret the Gospel narrative from the perspective of "myth fulfillment?" How are we to approach a story that represents the historical realization of the pagan myths of the dying and rising god, yet also points to something beyond history itself, to a transcendent world where Christ now dwells in his glorified humanity?

How are we to understand a narrative that points to the glorified Christ living in the members of his Mystical Body, the Church both on earth and in the heavens? How are we to digest a story that points at one and the same time to both the Jesus of History *and* the Christ of Faith and insists that the two are one?

One possible answer to these questions is to retrieve the patristic approach to Biblical interpretation that involved the four senses of Scripture: the literal, the tropological (or moral), the allegorical, and the anagogical. Rooted in the Platonic and Neoplatonic idea that universal ideas embody ultimate reality, and that these ideas have immersed themselves in the material world through various patterns that can be discerned by the human mind, this approach to Scripture recognizes the literal or historical sense of the Gospel narrative, but also maintains that there are deeper spiritual meanings that can be found by identifying parallel patterns of thought existing across the Scriptures or that coincide with the tradition of the Church. The historical-critical method would generally call this approach to interpreting Scripture *eisegesis* rather than authentic *exegesis* (that is, reading *into* Scripture rather than drawing out of it) because it embraces a nominalist understanding of reality that particulars alone exist and that ideas themselves are nothing but creations of the human mind. From a Platonic or Neoplatonic perspective, however, the allegorical approach is authentic exegesis since the patterns themselves participate in the realm of Ideas and are therefore just as real (if not more) than any text, whatever its historical setting or context.

Augustine once said, "For now treat the Scripture as the face of God. Melt in its presence."[10] God speaks to us through the Scriptures. He does so through his Spirit, who guides us to discern the pattern hidden within its various books and to apply them to our own lives. Because the magisterium of the Catholic is the official interpreter of Divine Revelation as found in both Scripture and Tradition, these patterns, hidden within Scripture, must

---

[10] Augustine of Hippo, *Sermon* 22.7. Cited in Robert Louis Wilken, *The Spirit of Early Christian Thought: Seeking the Face of God* (New Haven; Yale University Press, 2003), 50.

themselves coincide with its teachings. According to Thomas Aquinas, the spiritual senses of Scripture must be rooted in the literal (or historical sense): "Thus in Holy Writ no confusion results, for all the senses are founded on one—the literal—from which alone can any argument be drawn."[11] The spiritual senses, in other words, presuppose the literal and can add nothing to the literal required for salvation. While these senses may not contribute anything to the dogmatic content of the faith, they can deepen our understanding of the mysteries of the Christian faith and provide spiritual nourishment leading to a deeper encounter with God. According to Thomas Merton, "There is a difference between a mystery and a dogma. A dogma of the faith is a more abstract, authoritative statement of the truth to be believed in its official formulation….A mystery is not just the distilled and decanted formulation of revealed truth…in the

---

[11] Thomas Aquinas, *Summa theologiae*, I, q. 1, a. 10, ad 1.

mysteries of the faith we see God Himself."[12] The spiritual senses go deeper into the mystery of God's Word. To understand this insight better, the image of the cross comes to mind. The *literal* (historical) with its emphasis to the past and the *allegorical* that looks ahead to Christ's presence in his Mystical Body, the Church, corresponds to the horizontal beam. The *moral* (tropological) looking down into the depths of our human makeup and the *anagogical* pointing upward to the heavenly corresponds to the vertical beam. Together, they reflect the fullness of the mystery Christ's redemptive action, which embraces not only the historical and dogmatic, but also the spiritual and mystical. In the words of Augustine of Denmark: "The Letter speaks of deeds; allegory to faith; the Moral how to act; anagogy our destiny."[13] Let us now examine each of the four senses in a bit more detail.

---

[12] Thomas Merton, *Spiritual Direction ad Meditation* (Collegeville, MN: The Liturgical Press, 1987), 93=94.

[13] "Littera gesta docet, quid credas allegoria, moralis quid agas, quid speras anagogia." The Pontifical Biblical Commission, *The Interpretation of the Bible in the*

The Literal Sense. For much of the Church's history, the literal meaning of the text was taken at face value and identified with the historical. As we have seen, with the development of the historical-critical method, this identity between the literal and historical was brought into question. Much greater emphasis was then placed on interpreting the literal level of the text within its historical setting or *sitz im leben.* To do this, various subdisciplines were developed: textual criticism, source criticism, literary criticism, form criticism, redaction criticism —to name but a few. Because of these developments, the work involved in understanding the literal meaning of the text greatly expanded, and the attempt to situate the text within the confines of its actual historical context became much more complex. Still, the literal (or historical) meaning of the text, difficult as it may be to situate, remains the primary point of departure for interpreting the spiritual senses that presuppose it and rely on it.

Church (Vatican City: Libreria Editrice Vaticana, 1993), 78.

The Allegorical Sense. Those patterns in the Scriptural narrative relating to Christ and his Church pertain to the allegorical sense. Such parallels can pertain to Christ's relationship within the Godhead, the relationship between his divine and human natures, his redemptive mission, his incarnation, his public ministry, his passion and death, resurrection and ascension into heaven, the gift of his Spirit, the birth of the Church, his presence in the Church, his Mystical Body, in its pilgrim journey through time, and many more. As stated above, the allegorical sense must be rooted in the literal and provides spiritual nourishment for those who immerse themselves in the Scripture. Typical examples of the allegorical sense would be Moses lifting up the bronze serpent to heal the Jewish people who had been bitten by fiery serpents for their grumbling and lack of faith (Num 21:6-9) and the lifting up of Christ on the cross to heal the sins of humanity (Jn 3:14). Another parallel would Moses (representing the Old Law) leading his people (representing the Church out of Egypt), crossing the Red Sea (representing the sacrament of Baptism), wandering the desert (representing our pilgrim journey on earth) , and finally Joshua leading them into the Promised Land (representing our heavenly destiny). Such parallels break open the doctrinal message rooted in the literal text and show how reading God's Word provides spiritual nourishment for the faithful.

The Moral (or Tropological) Sense. Those patterns in Scripture that reveal something about the various levels of our human makeup—the physical, the intellectual, the psychological, the spiritual, and the social—concern the moral (or tropological) sense. This anthropological sense enables us to encounter Scripture in a way that allows the Word of God to intimately connect with our own real-life circumstances. It sheds light on the kind of people we are called to be, as well as the various ways in which we have fallen short of that goal. It helps us recognize the gap between vision and reality, and inspires us to take a good, hard look at ourselves and to ask ourselves if that gap is getting larger or smaller. An example of a moral interpretation of Scripture is Jesus' parable of the weeds and the wheat (Mt 13:24-33). The weeds sown by the enemy is likened to the evil we encounter inside ourselves, while the wheat stands for all the good within us. Rather than simply uprooting the weeds and running the risk of uprooting some of the wheat, the farmer lets the two grow together until harvest. At that time, the weeds are separated from the wheat and thrown into the fire. The wheat, in turn, is gathered into the farmer's barn. The kingdom of heaven is among us but also within us (Lk 17:21), This interpretation of the parable focuses on the latter. It says that our human imperfections will coexist in varying degrees with our deep yearning to be free of sin and live life in the Spirit. It will only be separated and finally purged when we stand in judgment before God our Maker.

The Anagogical Sense. The old creation has its destiny in the new. Jesus, the Second Adam, is the firstborn of the new creation. He became one of us so that we might be freed of the bonds of sin and share in this transformation of the old. The analogical sense uncovers those patterns within Scripture that point to the end times and our hope of one day sharing in God's divine life. It is eschatological in nature and deals in the "already-but-not-yet" of Jesus' Gospel message. It points to the world beyond, places the last things (death, judgment, heaven, hell) before our eyes, and reminds us that our human destiny lies beyond the pale of death. One of the three things that last, along with faith and love (1 Cor 13:13), hope helps us to keep our eyes on our end in God. Its opposites are presumption, which commits sin in anticipation that God's abundant grace will redeem us without our doing anything, and despair, which believes that God's grace is inaccessible to the sinner. While the former is a false hope, the latter is devoid of hope. The authentic hope, revealed by the anagogical sense, points to God's abundant grace, while at the same time requiring that we cooperate with that grace for it to achieve its intended effect. One example of an analogical interpretation of Scripture is to say that Moses' parting of the Red Sea (Ex 12:21) and leading the Chosen People out of the slavery of Egypt and into the Promised Land point to Jesus' redemptive mission to bring us out of the slavery of sin and lead us to heaven and the freedom of being his specially chosen sons and daughters. Another is seeing David's slaying of Goliath (1 Sm 17:1-58) as pointing to the ultimate triumph of good over evil, even amid seemingly insurmountable odds.

These four senses complement rather than conflict with one another. They offer a way of probing the deeper meanings of God's Word so it can be pondered and prayed over in a way that has deep personal relevance for the lives of the faithful. They see God as the primary author of Scripture who has hidden certain patterns of meaning in Scripture that lie beneath the literal sense. It also presupposes a canonical approach to Scripture, as it asserts that individual texts should be read not only in the light of their particular historical context, but also in view of the entirety of God's revealed Word. These senses help us to take Augustine's words to heart when he says that the Scriptures are the face of God and that we should melt in its presence.

Conclusion

To get the most meaning out of Christ's Gospel narrative, we must consider *all* the senses of Scripture: the literal, allegorical, moral, and anagogical. Christianity is not merely about setting the Biblical texts in their historical context or, as important as it may be, conveying abstract dogmatic principles to the faithful. It is also about pondering them in such a way that they reveal profound spiritual truths to the readers and enable them to listen as God speaks to their hearts through the text and invites them to enter a deeper, more intimate relationship with him.

Approaching Scripture by means of the four senses presupposes a continuity between the Jesus of History and the Christ of Faith. It affirms that Christ's Gospel narrative represents the fulfillment of the ancient pagan mythologies of the dying and rising god. Those myths were a remote preparation for the coming of Christ, the one and only dying and rising God, the myth that has become fact. It posits that our all-powerful God not only created the universe but was also capable of entering the world he created to become one of us. He did so not only to redeem us so that our sins might be forgiven, but also to elevate and transform us so that we might be able to share in the intimacy of the divine love. He became human so that we might become divine. He also became human so that he could experience the goodness of his creation from the inside out.

If Christ came to this earth so that God could experience his creation from the inside out, he also came so that humanity could experience divinity from the outside in. Interpreting Scripture through the lenses of the various senses enables us to understand both mysteries: that of the Word of God's incarnation in Jesus of Nazareth and humanity's redemption and ultimate divinization through Christ's Mystical Body. As important as it is, however, interpreting Christ's Gospel narrative is simply not enough. Much more is needed. It must not only be interpreted but also embraced. Such is the subject of our next chapter.

Christ's Gospel Narrative

- How do you view the relationship between the Jesus of History and the Christ of Faith?
- Which way of interpreting Christ's Gospel narrative do you agree with: the demythologizing approach or the myth fulfillment approach?

- How does the literal meaning of Scripture relate to Christ's Gospel narrative?
- How do the various spiritual senses relate to Christ's Gospel narrative?
- How would you describe your approach to interpreting Christ's Gospel narrative?

Prayer

Lord, help me to interpret your Gospel narrative. Help me ponder it in the light of your Spirit.

Chapter Three

Embracing Christ's Gospel Narrative

What does it mean to embrace Christ's Gospel narrative? Knowing just what it is and being able to interpret it are fine as far as they go. But God asks something more of us. He beckons to take this story of Gospel and make it our own. He wants us to make it an intimate part of our lives. He gave us this narrative to heal us but also to elevate and transform us. For that to happen, however, we must identify with this narrative and allow it to be the guiding principle of our lives. We must be willing to let go of our desire to shape our own destiny and allow God to step in and do it for us. He does this when we open our hearts to Christ and his message of God's unconditional and unfailing love for us and allow him to send his Spirit into our hearts and dwell within us. When this happens, we end up living an adventurous journey that will take us to places we never dreamed of or thought possible. Embracing Christ's Gospel narrative means living a life of continual conversion along the three-fold way of purgation, illumination, and union. It means taking up our cross daily and follow Christ along this path, so he may lead us to the Father and enjoy with him a life of heavenly glory.

A Life of Conversion

To follow Jesus with our whole mind, soul, and heart means to walk along the path of conversion. The word "conversion" (*metanoia* in Greek) means "to turn around." It means turning away from our life of egoism and self-centeredness, opening our hearts, and looking to Jesus. He wishes to enter into a deep, intimate relationship with each one of us, but he cannot do so if we refuse to let go of our petty wants and desires and allow him to fill us with his live and dwell within us. "The kingdom of God is within you," the Gospels say (Lk 17:21). That very same verse can be translated, "The kingdom of God is within your midst." Jesus is referring to himself as the Word-made-flesh who dwells *among* us, but also to himself as the Word-made-flesh who dwells *within* us. He wishes to befriend us (Jn 15:15) but cannot do so, if we do not wish to be befriended. For this to happen, we must reciprocate his invitation to enter into a deep personal relationship with him by turning away from our lives of narrow self-seeking, turn to him, look into his eyes, and open our hearts, and ask him quite honestly and unabashedly to enter into our hearts. Once we do so, our lives will never again be the same.

One of the most touching conversion stories in all of Scripture is Jesus' parable of the prodigal son (Lk 15:11-32). A father has two sons, and the younger sons asks for his share of the inheritance (normally this would be paid out after the father's death, so the son is saying, in effect, "you are dead to me."). The father gives his younger son his rightful share, and he proceeds to squander it on loose, dissolute living, so much so that he ultimately realizes that his father's servants were being fed far better than the pods that the pigs were eating. He resolves to return to his father and repent. He even rehearses what he was going to say: "I am no longer worthy to be called your son; treat me like one of your hired hands." (L 15:19). And so, the son makes his way home. On seeing him off in the distance, the father rushes out to the son in joyful celebration. He says, "Quickly, bring out a robe—the best one—and put it on him; put a ring on his finger and sandals on his feet. And get the fatted calf and kill it and let us eat and celebrate; for this son of mine was dead and is alive again; he was lost and is found! And they began to celebrate" (Lk 15:23-24). When the elder brother hears what has happened, he refuses to participate in the celebration because he feels he has been short-changed. He confronts the father and tells him that he was always faithful to him and never once was he given a feast in celebration of his loyalty. He remains stubborn and refuses to enter the house and join in the celebration. His father, in turn, goes out to him as says, "Son, you are always with me, and all that I have is yours. But we had to celebrate and rejoice, because this brother of yours was dead and has come to life; he was lost and has been found" (Lk 1531-32). Notice that the younger son has turned around (that is, converted) while we don't really know what the elder son will do. There is a bit of the younger and elder son in each of us. Jesus is calling us to turn to the Father. Rather than being called "The Parable of the Prodigal Son," perhaps the better for the parable would be "The Parable of the Merciful Father."

"Be perfect, therefore, as your heavenly Father is perfect" (Mt 5:48). Jesus calls us to walk along the path of holiness. For most of us, this is a lifelong process of successes and failures, triumphs and defeats, glories and heartaches. The life of conversion must be chosen time and time again, day after day, moment by moment. It involves not one decision but many. The prodigal son's journey home was long and arduous. To reach his destination, he had to remember where he was going and place one foot in front of the other, one step at a time. Jesus asks us to go and do likewise. Like the prodigal son, our return home, our radical change of heart, our fundamental option for Christ, must flow from our heart and manifest itself concretely in our daily lives. Our journey home involves countless daily decisions that nudge us closer to our heavenly destiny. It may take us a lifetime to get there (perhaps even more), but it will be well worth the time and effort.

The Three-fold Way

For most of us, conversion of heart is a lifelong process. Jesus tells us that the pure of heart will see God (Mt 5:8), but the sad fact of the matter is that most of us have impure and divided hearts. Because of humanity's fall from grace, our minds are darkened, our wills weakened, and our passions out of sync. Our spiritual visioned is blurred. We are spiritually nearsighted and easily give in to the temptations that promise us immediate gratification. Because of our weakened and wounded state, the journey from having a divided heart to a united one, from a heart filled to the brim with dirt to one that radiates light, is long and painful. Progress in the spiritual life involves pulling out the roots of sin that have grown deep into the ground of souls. Forsaking sin and seeking holiness requires patience, longsuffering, prayer, and a heartfelt recognition of our need for God's grace. For most of us, the journey to holiness takes a lifetime and continues after death. We need to be purged of our sins before we can be illumined by God's grace and united to him in love. It is for this reason that the Church speaks of the three-fold way of purgation, illumination, and union. [14]Let us look a bit closer at each of these stages of our pilgrim journey.

The Purgative Way. According to St Alphonsus de Liguori, "If a crystal vase is filled with earth, the rays of the sun cannot penetrate it. The light of God cannot illumine a heart that is full of attachments for the joys, the pleasures, and the honors of this world."[15] A soul full of earthly pleasures and concerns will not be able to allow the light of God's grace to shine in and do its work. At the beginning of our spiritual journey (as at every stage), we are called to do good and avoid evil. At the very outset, we do this by trying our best to observe the commandments (Ex 20:1-17; Dt 5:6-21) and avoid the allures of the Evil One. We soon find out, however, that doing so is easier said than done. We find ourselves falling time and time again and soon come to

---

[14] See *The New Dictionary of Catholic Spirituality,* ed. Michel Downey (Collegeville, MN: The Liturgical Press, 1993), s.v. "Three Ways" by Thomas D. McGonigle, O.P.

[15] Alphonsus de Liguori, *The School of Christian Perfection*, chap. 10.

see that we need God's help at every step of the way. Because we are beginners in the spiritual life and inexperienced in the ways of prayer, we open our hearts to God in prayer using traditional vocal prayers such as the Our Father, the Hail Mary, and the Glory Be. We also attend Mass on Sunday to fulfill our obligation to worship the Lord on the Sabbath. At this stage of our journey, the commandments are like an external scaffolding on a building that is necessary to repair it and possibly even prevent it from collapsing. This stage of the spiritual life focuses on cleansing us of our sins and obeying the commandments. Through the external disciplines of prayer, fasting, and almsgiving, it seeks to follow the Law and employs heartfelt repentance whenever it fails to do so. Those of us in the purgative stage are beginners in the spiritual life. We are not meant to stay there but to move on the next stage of our spiritual journey. As our relationship with the Lord deepens, we may experience periods of spiritual dryness in our lives. The consolations that often mark the beginning of our spiritual journey have disappeared, and we must rely on perseverance in our faith rather than our feelings. What is sometimes called "the dark night of the senses" may indicate that we are moving on to another stage in our spiritual sojourn.

The Illuminative Way. The purgative stage eventually leads to the illuminative, where the focus is on internalizing the commandments and living the life of virtue. The external supports of the previous stage are internalized. As a skeleton gives structure and definition to a body, enabling it to move from place to place on its own power, so do the virtues—both theological (faith, hope, charity) and cardinal (prudence, justice, fortitude, temperance)—enable us to keep the commandments as if doing so were a second nature to us. In the illuminative stage, we allow the light of Jesus Christ, the Word-made-flesh, to cast out whatever darkness is in our souls and enlighten our hearts and minds with the radiance of Divine Wisdom. We begin to see everything in the light of God's providential design and understand that time is immersed in the mystery of God's timelessness. We have internalized the faith to such an extent that our minds are enlightened, our wills strengthened, and our passions are getting more and more ordered. Although we still pray vocally, mental prayer (meditation) is our primary way of prayer. Through it, we cultivate the life of virtue and flee from the seven deadly vices of pride, avarice, envy, wrath, lust, gluttony, and sloth. We have not left the purgative way behind but have incorporated in our lives so that it itself has been transformed into a deeper and truer version of itself. Although we are now proficient in the spiritual life, we still have much to learn. The way of illumination is not a mere matter of seeing and understanding more fully the truths of the faith, but of seeing God's providential hand in all that happens and seeking to respond accordingly to the circumstances in which we find ourselves. We not only believe that God is everywhere, but we also begin to see his mysterious presence in the warp and woof of our daily lives. At this stage of our spiritual journey, our spiritual eyes are opened through the influence of God's grace, and we can discern with greater confidence the direction our lives are taking and the steps we need to find our way to God. At the same time, we may begin to experience doubts about the very nature of our faith and perhaps even the existence of God himself. Many saints such as Thérèse of Lisieux and Mother Teresa of Calcutta have experienced such moments of intense spiritual desolation, what is also known as "the dark night of the soul."

The Unitive Way. As the purgative stage leads to the illuminative, so does the illuminative lead to that of union. At some point in our spiritual journey, our heightened sense of God's awareness in our lives gives way to deep sense of living in communion with him. We discover that, while we have been trying to find our way to God, he all the while has been finding his way to us. Here, the emphasis is not on the commandments or the life of virtue, but on the ways of the Spirit. In this stage, we are so closely united to God that the various gifts and fruits of the Spirit are clearly manifest in our lives. That is not to say that the commandments and virtues are left beyond. Rather, it means that we are able to keep them assiduously, spontaneously, and with little effort because the Holy Spirit is at work in our lives and empowering us to do things we never would have thought possible. In this stage, we have become so transparent to God's love that the gifts of the Spirit—wisdom, understanding, counsel, knowledge, fortitude, piety, fear of the Lord—are fully manifest in our lives and the fruits of the Spirit—love, joy, peace, patience, kindness, goodness, faithfulness, gentleness, self-control—radiate out from us and touch others in ways that build up God's kingdom. The unitive stage leads us into mystical prayer, to which each of us is called, either in this life or in the next. We identify so deeply with God that we cannot distinguish ourselves from him, even though our creaturely status remains. Rather than merely conforming our wills with God's, we make ourselves one (uniform) with it.

It would be wrong to view the three stages of the threefold way in a linear fashion or to think that one stage is left behind rather than incorporated into the next as the spiritual journey continues. It would also be a mistake to think that we never go through the previous stages again during one's spiritual journey. The unitive way, in other words, presupposes and includes the illuminative way, while the illuminative presupposes and includes the purgative. Since each stage is incorporated into the succeeding one, it is also important to remember that the process of purgation continues in the illuminative stage and the illuminative continues in the unitive. Rather than viewing the three stages linearly, a better, more useful way of looking at them would be as an upward-moving spiral, one that starts at the bottom and moves up in a large circular fashion and forming smaller and smaller circular spirals until it reaches the top and comes to a single point. The point here is that we go through various moments of purgation, illumination, and union throughout our spiritual journey and in such a way that it deepens our relationship with God.

The Way of Holiness

The threefold way is just another way of talking about the call to holiness. God calls each of us to enter into an intimate friendship with him, the marks of which are benevolence, reciprocity, and mutually indwelling.[16] God wishes us well but actively seeks our well-being. He asks us to open our hearts to him as he opens his heart to us. He wants to dwell within our hearts and us to dwell within his. The way of holiness is all about the way of friendship. Jesus says to his disciples, "I do not call you servants any longer, because the servant does not know what the master is doing; but I have called you friends, because I have made known to you everything that I have heard from my Father" (Jn 15:15). Intimacy is a function of two things: self-disclosure and loving attention.[17] Jesus tells his disciples that he has made known to them everything that he has heard from his Father. He also gives them his complete and undivided attention. If we are to reciprocate in this invitation of friendship, we must disclose to Jesus the deepest secrets of our heart, even the hidden ones, those we are ashamed of and are afraid to bring out in the open.

---

[16] Paul J. Wadell, *Friendship and the Moral Life* (Notre Dame: University of Notre Dame Press, 1989), 130-41.

[17] Pat Collins, *Intimacy and the Hungers of the Heart* (Dublin: Columba Press, 1991), 104-43.

We must also spend time with him in prayer in the quiet of our hearts. Friends like to be in each other's company. They like to spend time together. They nourish their friendship in this way. They rest in each other's company. They even waste time together, for it is their friendship that matters, not what they accomplish or accumulate in their time together.

Friendships, of course, need to be fostered; otherwise, they are in danger of growing stale and ultimately becoming undone. By entering our world, suffering and dying for us, becoming nourishment for us, and a source of hope for us, Jesus has done his part. We, in turn, must do ours. We foster our relationship with him by trying our best to make his narrative our own. We know we cannot do this on our own and that we need his help. For this reason, the best way we can foster our relationship with him is through constant prayer. The Apostle Paul tells us, "Rejoice always, pray without ceasing, give thanks in all circumstances; for this is the will of God in Christ for you" (1 Th 5:16-18). Prayer is to the spiritual life what breathing is to physical life. We cannot live without it. The mystery behind it all is that prayer is not something that we do by ourselves, but it is itself a gift from God. Prayer requires faith, and faith itself is an infused gift from God. As St. Alphonsus de Liguori tells us, "Everyone receives sufficient grace to pray."[18] And again, "If you pray, you will be saved; if you do not pray, you will certainly be damned."[19] There is no great mystery to prayer. It is nothing else than simply talking to God, conversing with God as one friend to another. God already knows what's on our minds, but he wants to hear it from us.

There are many forms of prayer: vocal (talking to God out loud with words), mental (talking to God with words in the quiet of our hearts), and contemplative (wordless prayer, simply resting in God's presence without saying anything). When we turn to God in prayer, the important thing is to engage him on every level of our human makeup: the physical, emotional, intellectual, spiritual, and social. That is to say that we must find ways of

---

[18] Alphonsus de Liguori, *Prayer, the Great Means of Salvation*, 4.1

[19] Alphonsus de Liguori, *A Short Treatise on Prayer*, 6.

talking to him with our bodies, our feelings, our minds, our hearts, and our family and wider community. God wishes to relate to us on every level of our human makeup, not just the mind. He became one of us in the person of Jesus Christ so that we could do just that. The beauty of it all is that all these dimensions come together when we celebrate the Eucharist. When we gather for Mass, we worship God with our bodies though various signs and gestures. We engage the senses with colorful vestments, candles, incense, artwork. We engage the mind and heart when we listen to God's Word and hear the priest or deacon break the Word open for us so that it touches us, moves us, and strengthens us in our journey. When celebrated well, there are moments of quiet usually after the homily or after communion, when we simply sit together in silence and allow the Spirit of God to commune with us in silence. We also do it together, as a believing community, the family of God, the people of God. When we celebrate the Eucharist, we relate to God on every level of our human makeup. God enters our midst, dwells both within our hearts and in our midst, and his kingdom is made manifest.

Conclusion

To embrace Christ's Gospel narrative is to walk the along the path of holiness. Doing so means being willing to place the needs of others before our own and undergoing a process of continual, heartfelt conversion, one that seeks God's help in all things and allows him to purge us over time of our selfish concerns, enlighten our minds and hearts with the truth of God's Word, and make us one with Christ by virtue of the indwelling of his Spirit in our hearts. We are all called to conversion of heart and to walk along the path of holiness by taking up our cross daily to follow Jesus.

When we embrace Christ's Gospel narrative and make it our own, Christ embraces the narratives of our own lives and makes them his. He transforms the story of our lives into living Gospels. He does so by dwelling within our hearts and living his life through us. Jesus lives in and through the members of his body, the Church. This saying is not mere poetry or metaphor but a living reality. He lives within our hearts in a very real and tangible way by incorporating us into his glorified and risen existence. We live this glorified existence every time we enter the world of others, give ourselves to them completely, to become nourishment for them and a source of hope. "All the way to heaven is heaven," St. Catherine of Siena tells us.[20] When we embrace Christ's Gospel narrative, Christ himself embraces us and walks with us along the way of holiness.

Finally, it is important to note that prayer and holiness go hand in hand. We cannot become holy if we do not pray. Prayer itself is a gift from God that empowers us through his grace to relate to him on a very personal and intimate level. Prayer is to the spiritual life what breathing is to physical life. We are called to pray at all times, just as we must breathe at all times to get through the day. When we allow God to befriend us, he sends his Spirit to dwell in our hearts and intercedes for us. As St. Paul says, "…the Spirit helps us in our weakness; for we do not know how to pray as we ought, but

---

[20] Cited in Regis Martin, *The Last Things: Death, Judgment, Heaven, Hell* (San Francisco: Ignatius Press, 1998), 39.

that very Spirit intercedes with sighs too deep for words. And God, who searches the heart, knows what is in the mind of the Spirit, because the Spirit intercedes for the saints according to the will of God" (Rom 8:26-27). The Holy Spirit enables us not only to embrace Christ's Gospel narrative but also to live it. Living the Gospel message is the topic of our next chapter.

Christ's Gospel Narrative

- How do you view the process of conversion in your life?
- What purifications have you experienced?
- What light have you received?
- What experiences of communion with the Lord have you experienced?
- How have such experiences repeated themselves in your life?

Prayer

Lord, help me embrace your Gospel narrative in all its darkness and glory, no matter what the cost.

Chapter Four

Living Christ's Gospel Narrative

Jesus wants us to embrace his Gospel narrative so that it may take root in the depths of our hearts, flow through every aspect of our being, and spill over into our words and actions. He wants us not only to tell his story but live it. He wants us to make it our own in such a way so that with the Apostle Paul, we will be able to say, "…it is no longer I who live, but it is Christ who lives in me" (Gal 2:20). Christ wants to live in our hearts so that we might live in his. Because we live in a wounded world, however, we know deep down inside that we cannot do this on our own. Try as we may to do otherwise, left to our resources, we will gradually change the focus of Christ's Gospel narrative to make it conform to our own selfish desires. To live this narrative as it was meant to be lived, we need the grace of the Holy Spirit. Only with his divine assistance will his gifts and fruits become manifest in our lives. Only with this heavenly aid at work deep within our hearts will we live according to the values of the beatitudes taking root in the world around us.

Our Wounded World

We all sense that things are not right with the world, that somewhere we have wandered off course and that the present reality is not the way God had originally intended it. Perhaps he foresaw what would happen when he created our world, that human beings endowed with free will with the capacity to reciprocate his love for them could also refuse to do so and go their own way. If he foresaw this (and his presumed omniscience suggests he did), one possible explanation of his creating us the way he did is that he knew that a greater good would come out of our human errancy. God, according to this line of reasoning, created us, knowing all the while that we would reject him to follow our own selfish ambitions. To rewrite the wrong initiated by our first parents, he entered our world in the person of Jesus Christ, gave of himself completely to us, and became nourishment for us and a perennial source of hope. Before we immerse ourselves in the mystery of what he has done, we must first examine the contours of our wounded nature, embrace what we have discovered, and humbly place our wounds before the Lord our God.

Jesus came to redeem our wounded world and transform our fallen humanity. According to the *Catechism of the Catholic Church*, "The account of the fall in *Genesis* 3 uses figurative language, but affirms a primeval event, a deed that took place *at the beginning of the history of man*. Revelation gives us the certainty of faith that the whole of human history is marked by the original fault freely committed by our first parents."[21] The story of the Fall, in other words, presents in symbolic language an actual event that happened at the dawn of human existence. The sin of our first parents was a sin of human nature. Their descendants did not commit this sin but contracted it and its consequences. Since the term, *Adam*, can refer both to the collective whole (the entire human race) and a single person (the first primate into whom God breathed an immortal rational soul), it is possible that at the

---

[21] *Catechism of the Catholic Church*, no. 390.

creation of man and woman humanity enjoyed a kind of collective consciousness that gave them a deep awareness of their interrelated nature. Vestiges of such a consciousness can be seen in nature when we look at the way a colony of ants or a swarm of bees works together. Something may very well have been true of our early forebears.

Because Adam and Eve represented the summit of God's creative action, their fall from grace affected not only them and their ancestors but the whole of creation. Their sin had a ripple effect on the entire universe. Because of it, creation was thrown into a state of discord. The forces of Nature ceased to function as originally intended. Although they still maintained a resemblance to their pristine state and purpose, an element of uncertainty was thrown into their way of functioning. They fell out of harmony with each other and tended toward disarray. The upward (anabolic) pull of Nature was countered by a downward (catabolic) movement toward corruption and decay. Although God's material creation was not totally corrupted, it had fallen far below God's plan for it and was destined to be a threat and a danger to human existence. The casting of Adam and Eve out of the Garden of Eden reflects Creation's wounded and corrupted nature. From now on, man would have to work the land by the sweat of his brow and woman would suffer the pain of labor when giving birth.

Adam and Eve's fall from grace also had concrete consequences for humanity. Not only did we lose contact with the group consciousness that tied us together as a collective whole, but our minds were darkened, our wills weakened, and our passions, originally ordered to follow the gentle rule of reason's reign, fell badly out of sync with each other and with reason itself. Although our human nature was not totally corrupted, it was deeply wounded and could no longer open itself to the divine. Left to ourselves and without the help of divine grace, there was little hope that we would survive in a world wounded by our own selfish and sinful ways. The sin of our first parents made us susceptible to committing our own personal sins. The story of Cain and Abel (Gn 4:1-16) shows how, once unleashed, envy and jealousy could wreak havoc even our family and other personal ties. The Story of the Tower of Babel (Gn 11:1-9), moreover, shows how the structures we created would themselves be sinful, precisely because they were made by us. Hence the rise of social sin. The only solution to humanity's dilemma was for God to intervene and rebuild creation from the inside out. Christ's Gospel narrative was God's chosen way of making things right. Through the God-man's passion, death, and resurrection, original sin was forgiven, humanity's fellowship with God was restored, and we could resume our principal vocational task of finding our way to God.

Our Spiritual Journey

We were created to be in intimate communion with God, the ground of our being and source of all that exists. If that fellowship was disrupted by humanity's primeval fall from grace, it was eventually restored by God through his sending his Son to redeem us by entering our world, giving himself to us completely, becoming nourishment for us, and remaining for us a source of hope. Jesus' Incarnation, Passion and Death, Eucharistic meal, and Resurrection say everything there is to say about Christ's

Gospel narrative which, when all is said and done, is meant to become our own. The contours of this narrative come from the mouth of Jesus himself, when he said to his disciples, "If any want to become my followers, let them deny themselves and take up their cross and follow me" (Mk 8:34). To carry the cross, we must enter Jesus' world, give ourselves to him completely, become nourishment for him as he is nourishment for us, and a source of hope for all those who are members of his body, the Church.

There is an eschatological, "already-but-not-yet," dimension to Christ's Gospel narrative as it relates to the concrete circumstances of our daily lives. While he himself has lived this narrative, we ourselves are trying to do so, and there is always (at least in this lifetime) a gap between our living out of this narrative to the fullest and the false narratives that tend to govern our lives. The spiritual journey is all about recognizing the gap between the persons we are called to become and the flawed human beings we actually are. In whatever circumstances we find ourselves, we need to recognize that gap, determine how wide it is, and honestly ask ourselves if our daily actions and lifestyles are contributing to making the gap larger or smaller. In other words, are we striving to make our way to become the persons God has envisioned us to be, or are we turning ourselves into something less than that vision, something that denigrates our true worth as human beings and is an offense to our human dignity?

In the Christian tradition, the spiritual journey must be rooted in faith, hope, and love, what theologians refer to as the theological virtues. Every journey has a destination. For the Christian, that goal is heaven, that is, seeing God face to face in the beatific vision. The *visio Dei* is the source of all human happiness. Since God cannot be empirically verified, we must rely on faith that God does indeed exist. Without faith in the very existence of our ultimate end, there would be no reason for starting out in the first place. Similarly, all along the journey we must have hope of one day getting there. Life has all sorts of obstacles and distractions, and we often let them get in the way. We take a wrong turn, then another, and another. Sometimes, we may even feel lost and be tempted to give up the journey altogether. The virtue of hope prevents us from one of two extremes: despair of our ever finding our way to God and the presumption that heaven is simply ours for the asking and little or no effort is required on our part to get us there. The former embodies no hope, while the latter embraces a false hope. True hope recognizes that, if we wish to one day see him face to face, we must look to God at every step of our journey. Finally, the virtue of love involves all the little things we do in planning and preparing for our journey. Since we are social beings by nature, we normally journey to God in groups of family, friends, parish communities, and the like. We travel together and help each other out as we navigate the difficult earthly and spiritual terrain between where we are and where we are aiming to go. For most (if not all) of us, there is always a gap between where we presently are in the spiritual life and where God wants us to go. The key question we must constantly ask ourselves and one another is if that gap between vision and reality is getting larger or smaller. For most of us, the gap is somewhat erratic, at times getting narrower and narrower; at other times getting bigger and bigger.

Only prayer, what St. Alphonsus de Liguori calls "a necessary and certain means of obtaining salvation,"[22] enables us to remain firmly rooted in faith, hope and love, so that we stay focused on our destination and persevere in our getting there.

Prayer is to the spiritual life what breathing is to our earthly life. The Apostle Paul tells us to "pray without ceasing" (1 Th 5:17). This verse has been variously interpreted as praying the psalms at various moment of the day in order to sanctify it, offering up our good actions of the day in a morning offering, recognizing that the Holy Spirit yearns within us crying out "Abba, Father" (Rom 8:15), and saying the Jesus Prayer over and over until it becomes a constant refrain of our hearts. It also means that we are called to engage the Lord on every level of our human makeup—the physical, emotional, intellectual, spiritual, and social—and that we must find the right rhythm in our lives that, in some way during the day, turns to each of these levels (albeit at different times and in different

---

[22] Alphonsus de Liguori, *Prayer, The Great Means of Salvation*, Introduction.

ways). Prayer also enables us to persevere in the purgative, illuminative, and unitive stages of our spiritual journey, in what the spiritual masters often refer to as the three-fold way.

Living Christ's Gospel Narrative

As we saw in the previous chapter, the three-fold way of purgation, illumination, and union is meant to play itself out in the concrete circumstances of our everyday lives. We empty ourselves to be transformed by the life of the virtues and ultimately by the Spirit of Christ himself. This process involves a gradual transformation of our very lives. As St. Paul reminds us, "You were taught to put away your former way of life, your old self, corrupt and deluded by its lusts, and to be renewed in the spirit of your minds, and to clothe yourselves with the new self, created according to the likeness of God in true righteousness and holiness" (Eph 4:22-24).

What does it mean to live Christ's Gospel narrative in this way? How can we take off the old self and put on the new? What does it mean to take up our cross daily and follow the way of the Lord Jesus? What follows are some practical suggestions for making the Gospel message a vivid reality in our own lives and in the lives of those we are called to serve.

Establish a regular pattern of daily prayer in your life. As mentioned earlier, prayer is to the spiritual life what breathing is to our physical, earthly lives. Just as it is impossible to go through a single day on a single breath, it is also impossible to find our way to God each day on a single prayer. We must take seriously the Apostle Paul's injunction to pray without ceasing and strive to make it a part of our daily routine. To do so, we can try to incorporate into our lives some of the interpretations of constant prayer outlined earlier in this chapter. We can also simply try to become more aware of God's presence in our lives and the way he walks before us to show us the way, behind us to catch us when we fall, beside us to accompany us in our journey, and within us to comfort us in times of distress. It is also important to set aside a particular time each day for personal prayer. The practice of making a regular holy hour where we can talk to God in the silence of our hearts or simply reset quietly in his presence is also highly recommended.

Read and meditate upon the Scriptures. St. Augustine once said, "For now treat the Scripture of God as the face of God. Melt in its presence."[23] God uses Scripture to speak to us personally and touch our hearts. For this to happen, we need to read it slowly and prayerfully in the style of *lectio divina* (holy reading). We should be focused not merely on the literal meaning of the text (important as it is) but also on its deeper spiritual meaning. If Scripture truly is the face of God, then we should approach it with the simple assumption that he wishes to speak to us through it. Since God speaks to us in the silence of our hearts, it is important for us to read Scripture in a meditative manner. Only then will the deep riches of God's word reveal themselves to us and take on practical significance for us in our daily lives. Although we must take care not to mistake God's voice for our own (hence the importance to be in accord with the teaching of the Church in matters of faith and morals), we seek to

---

[23] Augustine of Hippo, *Sermon* 22.7.

avoid the other extreme viewing God's Word as the exclusive domain of Scriptural exegetes and theologians. God's Word is meant for everyone's spiritual nourishment and growth and has significance for each of us as we seek to grow in holiness.

Frequent the sacraments of the Church. Because we are both physical and spiritual beings, God also speaks to us through concrete signs. It is said that Jesus himself is the sacrament of God, the Church is the sacrament of Christ, and the seven sacraments are the sacraments of the Church. These seven visible signs point of God's presence in our midst and are active conveyors of divine grace. They are actions of Christ mediated through the appointed ministers of the Church and are meant to strengthen us in our spiritual journey. As "the source and summit of Christian Life,"[24] the Eucharist is the sacrament of sacrament from which all others flow. There is a sacrament designed for every stage of our spiritual journey from beginning (baptism) to end (anointing of the sick and viaticum), from stepping into Christian maturity

---

[24] Second Vatican Council, *Lumen gentium*, no. 9.

(confirmation) to our vocational state (marriage, ordination), from repentance for our sins (reconciliation) to food for the journey (Eucharist). These visible signs are meant to accompany us at every stage of our journey, and it is important for us to frequent them and make them an integral part of our spirituality. To neglect the sacraments is to overlook one of the most significant helps God has given us for our spiritual sojourn.

Go to spiritual direction. At times, it is difficult for us to discern where the Lord is leading us during our earthly sojourn. We may have our end in sight but the way there seems fraught with various forks and turns in the road that make it unclear to us just what our next steps should be. At times like these, we may very well benefit from going to a trained spiritual director, someone who will help us unpack the story of our lives and assist us in discovering the places where that story and Christ's Gospel narrative coincide. A spiritual director listens to our story and reflects it back to us. Through a process of active listening, he or she helps us get in touch with our feelings about ourselves and our relationship with God and with others and express them in healthy and constructive ways. He or she then helps us get in touch with our various needs (large and small; spiritual and material) express them to God and find practical take-aways that will gradually move us closer to our desired end. A good spiritual director will help us listen to the voice of the Holy Spirit (our true spiritual director) and respond to his quiet promptings deep within our hearts.

Be an eager and willing servant. Jesus tells us that the greatest commandment is to love God with all our heart, mind, and soul, and that the second is to love your neighbor as yourself (Mt 22:37). The Apostle James tells us that we should manifest our faith through his works (Jas 2:18). One very practical way of serving others is by carrying out the corporal and spiritual acts of mercy. The corporal acts of mercy are as follows:

- To feed the hungry
- To give drink to the thirsty
- To clothe the naked
- To give shelter to the homeless
- To visit the sick

- To ransom the captive
- To bury the dead

The spiritual works of mercy, by way of contrast are:

- To instruct the ignorant
- To counsel the doubtful
- To admonish sinners
- To bear wrongs patiently
- To forgive offences willingly
- To comfort the afflicted
- To pray for the living and the dead[25]

Pope Francis tells us that Jesus is the face of the Father's mercy.[26] When we perform any one of these works of mercy, we are bringing Christ to others and putting his Gospel narrative into action. We ourselves bring the face of the Father's mercy to those in need and give flesh and bones to Christ's

---

[25] *Catechism of the Catholic Church*, no. 2447.

[26] Pope Francis, *Misericordiae vultus*, no. 1.

message of plentiful redemption to our wounded world.

Conclusion

Christ's Gospel narrative is meant not merely to be embraced but to be lived. This narrative takes root in our lives throughout our earthly sojourn in a gradual process of purgation, illumination, and union, one that takes a lifetime to unfold and for most of us continues to unfold even after death. The goal is simple and straightforward: The more Jesus' narrative becomes our own, the more he befriends us and allows his Spirit to dwell within our hearts. When Jesus' narrative becomes fully our own, we will identify ourselves so closely with him that we will hardly be able to distinguish between the two. With Paul, we will be able to say, "it is no longer I who lives, but it is Christ who lives in me" (Gal 2:20).

Making Christ's Gospel narrative our own is possible only through God's help, the grace of the Holy Spirit. We must cooperate with that grace, to be sure, but it is much more a divine work rather than a human work. When we make Christ's Gospel narrative our own, Christ, in turn, makes our narrative his. Rather than simply making our lives a carbon copy of his own, he tells his story through our stories, transforming them into beautiful tales of God's love of humanity and humanity's love of God. Christ's Gospel narrative, in other words, reveals to us the deepest meaning of our lives. He reveals to us the meaning of our own life narratives but showing their reflection in mystery of his own.

There is a close connection between Christ's Gospel narrative and the narratives of our own lives. God became one of us so that we one day might share in his divinity. While the distinction between the human and the divine, between the Creator and the created, never goes way, the intimate sharing of God's life with us is so profound that it is impossible to express in words the depths of God's dwelling within our hearts and our dwelling within his. This message needs to be shared and spread to all the corners of the earth and the deepest recesses of the human heart.

Christ's Gospel Narrative

- What is it like living in a wounded world?
- What are your wounds?
- How do you deal with them during your spiritual journey?
- What practical steps have you taken to deepen your spiritual life?
- What new steps is the Lord asking you to take?

Prayer

Heal me of my wounds, Lord. Show me the way to holiness and wholeness.

Chapter Five

Sharing Christ's Gospel Narrative

At the end of Matthew's Gospel, Jesus says to the eleven: "Go therefore and make disciples of all nations, baptizing them in the name of the Father and of the Son and of the Holy Spirit, and teaching them to obey everything that I have commanded you. And remember, I am with you always, to the end of the age" (Mt 28:19-20). The following of Christ is missionary by its very nature. Pope Francis, in fact, calls all Catholic Christians to be missionary disciples.[27] Although most of us would agree that evangelization should be foremost on our minds, a large disparity arises when deciding upon the best way to go about it. In this final chapter, we will look at how Jesus himself evangelized and his followers should follow suit.

---

[27] Pope Francis, *Evangelium Gaudium*, no. 120.

The Ministry of Jesus

The baptism of Jesus marks the start of his public ministry (Mk 1:1-14). He humbly submits to the John the Baptist, who immerses him in the Jordan, and the Spirit descends on him in the form of a dove with a voice from heaven saying, "You are my Son, the Beloved, with you I am well pleased" (Mk 1:11). This act sanctifies the waters of the Jordan and marks the institution of the sacrament of Baptism. In this symbolic action ("an outward sign instituted by Christ to give grace"[28]), the person being baptized is immersed in the paschal mystery of Jesus' passion, death, and resurrection, cleansed of original sin, and becomes an adopted son or daughter of God. When seen in this light, it becomes clear that the cross of Golgotha and the empty tomb of Easter morning define Jesus' public ministry mark from beginning to end. Like matching bookends, the paschal mystery opens Jesus' public ministry and closes it. Everything he does

---

[28] *The Baltimore Catechism*, no. 304.

during his ministry is oriented toward those final climactic moments of his life.

According to the Gospel of Mark, after Jesus' baptism, "…the Spirit immediately drove him out into the wilderness. He was in the wilderness forty days, tempted by Satan; and he was with the wild beasts; and the angels waited on him"(Mk 1:12-13). Notice that the Spirit is the force that moves him. Being in the wilderness, living among the wild beasts, and being tempted by Satan signify Jesus' struggle with evil. The wild beasts represent the passions, while the temptations of Satan stand for evil thoughts and inclinations planted in our minds by the Evil One. The Letter to the Hebrews tells us that in Jesus "…we have one who in every respect has been tested as we are, yet without sin" (Heb 4:15). Jesus overcomes these evil powers because he is moved by the Spirit and ministered to by angels. His time in the wilderness strengthens him for all that lies ahead.

When he leaves the wilderness after forty days, we see him as a Beloved Son with a clear vision and a firm purpose in carrying out the will of his Father in heaven. He goes to Galilee and proclaims the

Good News of God: "The time is fulfilled, and the kingdom of God has come near; repent, and believe in the good news" (Mk 1:15). He then gathers a group of disciples, the first four of whom are fishermen—Peter and Andrew; James and John—promising them that he would make them fishers of men (Mk 1:16-20). He then sets out on a mission of teaching, healing, driving out demons, performing miraculous feats that never had been witnessed by the people of the region. In time, he appoints an inner circle of twelve Apostles (Mk 3:13-19) and brings his ministry outside of Galilee (Mk 7:24-10:52) and eventually to Jerusalem itself (Mk 11:1-13:37). Throughout his public ministry he teaches mostly through parables (Mk 4:1-34; 12:1-12), heals a demoniac (Mk 1:21-28), a leper (Mk 1:40-45), a paralytic (Mk 2:1-12), a man with a withered hand (Mk 3:1-6), a woman with a hemorrhage (Mk 5:25-34), a young girl who was dead and is back to life (Mk 5:21-24, 35-43), a deaf man (Mk 7:31-37), a blind man (Mk 8:22-26), and an epileptic (Mk 9:14-29). He also performed such miracles of nature as the multiplication of the loaves and fishes (Mk 6:30-44; 8:1-10) and walking on water (Mk.

6:45-52). Throughout Mark's Gospel (and all the Gospels, for that matter), Jesus is depicted as someone who spoke with authority and had the power to command the forces of nature. He spread his Gospel message by telling his hearers that the kingdom of God was at hand, gathering an intimate circle of friends with whom he could share his ministry, teaching with authority, and healing the wounds of those he encountered. All his actions were focused on the defining moment of his life, when he would celebrate a final meal with his disciples (Mk 14:2-25) and offer his life for the deepest wounds of humanity—those that disfigured their spirits, souls, and bodies—so that they might be free of sin and arrive one day in the place he has prepared for them.

The Evangelizing Church

Jesus' actions during his own public ministry offer us some guidelines about how his followers should go about spreading the Good News. In the first place, Jesus humbled himself by being baptized by John in the Jordan. Christians should not put on condescending airs of superiority in their dealings with others. We are in no way worthy of the forgiveness we have received from Christ, and we should not act as if we were. Humility is the mark of a true disciple. Like Jesus, we are called to humble ourselves before God and others by emptying ourselves and being other-oriented rather than self-oriented. Jesus, moreover, instituted the sacrament of Baptism, and we should recognize the implications that receiving this sacrament has for our lives. In Baptism, we are immersed in Christ's paschal mystery and redeemed by its life-saving action. At Baptism, the Spirit descends on us, and the Father calls us his beloved sons and daughters. It reminds us that we need the grace of the Spirit to grow out of ourselves and turn toward others. For this reason, we should frequent the sacraments of the Church and ask God to help us to follow the way of the Lord Jesus in our daily lives.

For this to happen, the Spirit sometimes drives us into the wilderness to struggle with temptation and the wild allure of our untamed passions. The forty days of Lent remind us of Jesus' own forty-day sojourn in the wilderness and should inspire us to make prayer, fasting, and almsgiving an integral part of our lives. We are all called to delve deep into the wilderness of our hearts and confront whatever wounds and weaknesses we find there. God will not heal what we ourselves have not discovered, confronted, and openly shared with him. Moreover, like Jesus who was ministered to by angels during his time in the wilderness, we need to peer into the surrounding darkness, as well as the light that casts it out and shines upon the path we are to follow. We should not separate Jesus' time in the desert from his public ministry. If the Spirit drove Jesus into the wilderness, it follows that he also led him out of it and inspired him to gather a group of followers around himself and ask them to walk with him as he proclaimed the Good News of the coming of God's kingdom and his ministry of teaching and healing. Jesus, in other words, gathered a community around himself and invited them to join him in the work of sharing the Good News.

What does all this have to do with the way we are called to evangelize? What lessons can we learn from the way Jesus himself shared the Good News? How can we, his disciples, carry out his mission in today's world? If we wish to evangelize others, we ourselves need first to be evangelized. We need to establish a personal relationship with Jesus and respond to his call to follow him into the wilderness of our hearts, confront the darkness we find there, and allow the light of God's grace to cast it out. While there, we are also called to the practices of prayer, fasting, and almsgiving, so we may discern by the light of God's grace his plan for us in our lives. Evangelization, the sharing of the Good News, involves first and foremost, cultivating our friendship with Christ and sharing it with others. "I do not call you servants any longer...but I have called you friends" (Jn 15:15). Jesus wishes to be your closest, most intimate, friend. This is the message we need to get across in sharing the Good News. If we fail in communicating this basic, most fundamental, message, all catechetical programs we develop will fall far short of what Jesus is asking of and expecting from his followers.

Practical Suggestions for Sharing the Gospel Message

Given all the above, it is now time for us to list some practical suggestions for evangelizing as Christ and his earliest disciples did. These comments are not meant to be comprehensive. Their purpose is only to point us in the right direction for an effective sharing of the Gospel message.

To begin with, to share the Gospel effectively, we must be firmly grounded in our own faith. This requires a commitment on our part to root ourselves in the Scriptures and the teachings of the Church. We cannot share with others what we ourselves do not possess. Even more important than having a firm knowledge of the faith, it is also essential to talk to God from your heart so that your personal relationship with him will grow. The closer we come to Jesus, the more clearly will his life shine through us and influence our relationships with others. If we wish to draw others closer to Christ, we ourselves must do so. One of the problems in the Church today is that it has many lukewarm members, many of whom have little or no know-

ledge of the faith and little or no personal knowledge of Christ himself. "So, because you are lukewarm, and neither cold nor hot, I am about to spit
you out of my mouth" (Rv 3:16). These words from
the Book of Revelation remind us that Jesus wants
his disciples to be fervent followers.

Take Jesus' teaching on love to heart. Three say-
ings in particular come to mind.

1. "Jesus answered "The first commandment
   is 'Hear, O Israel: The Lord our God, the
   Lord is one; you shall love the Lord your
   God with all your heart, and with all your
   soul, and with all your mind, and with all
   your strength.' The second is this, 'You
   shall you've your neighbor as yourself'
   There is no other commandment greater
   than these" (Mk 12:29-31).

2. "I give you a new commandment, that you
   love one another. Just as I have loved you,
   you also should love one another. By this
   everyone will know that you are my disciples, if you love one another" (Jn 13:34-35).

3. "No one has greater love than this, to lay down one's life for one's friends" (Jn 15:13).

The love we bear for one another is not only a sign of Jesus' presence in our midst, but also one of the most effective means of sharing the Gospel message. Without such concrete expressions of love, the Gospel becomes stale and emptied of its transforming power.

Do not proselytize. Jesus' disciples are called to share their love for him and one another by the way they talk about him and live their lives. Sharing their faith with others should not be used as a tool to win them over to the faith. Doing so would be a misuse of the Gospel and a sign off disrespect for those with whom we are sharing. We share our faith out of our love for Jesus, not because we want to put another notch in our belt or mark in our Bibles to register another convert to the faith. People must always be free to accept the Gospel message or refuse it. Their choice should not be influenced by money, gifts, or services rendered. To proselytize others is to misunderstand the transforming nature of Jesus' message. He entered our world, gave himself completely to the point of dying for us, to become nourishment and a source of hope for us, because he loved us and wanted to free us from the bondage of sin and lead us to life in a new creation. He taught, healed, and cast out demons out of love for others and never used his power to force anyone in following him. Nor should we.

Build solid friendships with your fellow Christians, as well as with non-believers. Our friendship with Christ should spill over into our relationships with others. Although friendships with fellow believers will be different from those with those who do not believe in Christ (simply because we can talk more openly about our belief in Christ with our Christian friends), both are to be encouraged. In Christian friendship, Jesus is always a silent partner in our gatherings, since he himself once said, "[W]here two or three are gathered in my name, I am there among them" (Mt 18:20). With Jesus in our midst, we can deepen our relationship with Christ and grow in our love for one another one another. In our friendships with non-believers, there is no need to even mention Christ (unless they specifically bring it up). With them, we preach the Gospel primarily through the love we bear them. If Jesus is our friend and dwells in our hearts, then he will use us to touch our friends and move them in ways beyond all telling.

Participate in your faith community. As believers, we are part of Christ's Mystical Body, the Church, which is made of the Church triumphant (those in heaven), the Church penitent (those in purgatory), and the Church militant (those still on their earthly sojourn). As the sacrament of Christ, the Church has a concrete, visible manifestation on earth in the local believing community. We share the Gospel message and give witness to the presence of Christ in our midst in and through this body of believers. The witness of the local parish community can be a powerful tool of evangelization, one that often has a much greater impact that whatever witness we can give by ourselves. As "the Church in miniature," the family is called in a special way to participate in this corporate witness, as is the local parish community, the local diocese, and so on, all the way up to the Church universal. We must never overlook the importance of building up the faith of the local faith community as a way of giving witness to the Gospel message.

Invite someone to Sunday Mass with you. The institution of the sacraments of Baptism and Eucharist encompasses Jesus' public ministry, serving as bookends that define it and hold it in place. Baptism immerses a person in Christ's paschal mystery while the Eucharist brings that mystery into our midst whenever we celebrate it. Along with prayer and Scripture, the sacraments are the primary means by which we foster our friendship with Christ and receive the necessary graces to help us in our spiritual sojourn. Through them, we receive food for our journey and the forgiveness of whatever sins we might commit along the way. Not receiving them will only result in distancing ourselves from God, others, and our deepest, truest selves. As the sacrament of sacraments and the sacrament of love, the Eucharist, brings us into close contact with Jesus' passion, death, and resurrection. It shapes our minds and hearts by instructing us through the breaking open of God's Word and by giving us visible signs of God's presence in the world and in our lives. Think about inviting someone you know, love, and respect to attend Sunday Mass with you. After Mass, take your friend out for a meal and share with him or her why the Mass is so important to you. Do not be afraid of sharing with your friends what is dear to your heart.

Place everything in God's hands and trust that he is working not only through you, but through others, and most especially directly through his grace. God's grace is abundant and, as we have seen, everyone receives the grace to pray. We sometimes mistakenly think that we alone are solely responsible for spreading the Gospel message. We forget that we are members of the Christ's body and that, in the end, it is he (not us) who draws others to himself. We must bear in mind the words of St. Paul, "I planted, Apollos watered, but God gave the growth. So neither the one who plants nor the one who waters is anything, but only God who gives the growth. The one who plants and the one who waters have a common purpose, and each will receive wages according to the labor off each" (1 Cor 3:6-8). God is at work in everyone's life: believers and non-believers alike. He seeks us all out, at times, even despite ourselves and our efforts to avoid him. He does so, moreover, in his own due time: "…with the Lord one day is like a thousand years, and a thousand years are like one day. The Lord is not slow about his promise, as some think of slowness, but is patient with you, not wanting any to perish, but all to come to repentance" (2 Pt 3:8-9). We too must be patient in our sharing the Gospel message.

Conclusion

God calls everyone to share the Gospel message. We are called to do so as individuals but also as a community, especially in our families and local faith communities. Before we can evangelize others, we ourselves must be evangelized. Conversion (*metanoia*) involves a lifelong process of emptying our hearts of our selfish, worldly concerns and opening them up to the transforming presence of divine grace. Jesus commanded his disciples to preach the Gospel to the ends of the earth. At the same time, we must also recognize that the Gospel is ultimately meant to reach the farthest and most darkened corners of every human heart. The power of Jesus' words and actions, his teaching and miracles, continues to this day through the ministry of his body, the Church.

Sharing Christ's Gospel narrative involves following Jesus from his baptism in the Jordan to his passion and death on Golgotha, to his rising from the dead on Easter morning. His empty tomb is a symbol of his victory over death and his glorious triumph over the forces of evil that desecrate the world and are the scourge of the human heart. Through Baptism, we already share in the new, divinized, and glorified life that is to come, and eagerly await its fullness in the afterlife. As we anticipate its coming, we share the joy of the Gospel message with those around us by living our lives deeply rooted in the three things that last faith, hope, and love (1 Cor 13:13). The Gospel message is the story of God's love for us in the person of Jesus Christ. Whenever we love as Christ loved, we are sharing his Gospel message, because when doing so, it is Christ himself who is loving in us and through us.

Jesus always found practical ways of sharing the message of the coming of the kingdom. He told simple stories that were easy to understand yet ripe with meaning. He brought his message directly to the people by traveling as an itinerant preacher throughout the hill country, towns, and villages, of Galilee, Samaria, and Judea. He moved people's hearts through the authority of his words and healed them of their physical wounds and ailments by a simple touch of his hands and a firm command. We too are called to find practical means of sharing the Good News of our freedom from the bondage of sin to the new life won for us by Jesus' passion, death, and resurrection. We do so because we are Jesus' disciples, and he has asked us to follow him by sharing our love for him with others by the way we think, speak, and act. Sharing the Gospel message is simply a matter of allowing Jesus to live in us through the indwelling of his Spirit. If we open our hearts to him, he will go there, dwell there, and reach out to others in ways we never before thought possible.

Christ's Gospel Narrative

- How did Jesus evangelize?

- In what ways does the Church follow his example?
- In what ways does it not?
- How do you share Christ's Gospel message?
- What more can you do to share it?

Prayer

Help me, Lord, to share your Gospel message. Help me to love as you love.

Conclusion

"It is no longer I who live, but it is Christ who lives in me" (Gal 2:20). God entered our world in the mystery of the Incarnation, gave himself completely to us in the mystery of his Passion and Death, and became nourishment for us in the mystery of the Eucharist and a source of hope for us in the mysteries of his resurrection and ascension into heaven. This Gospel narrative represents a critical turning point of human history. It tells the true story of how Jesus freed us from the bondage of sin and is helping us even now find our way to the Father. Because of its central importance for our lives, this narrative needs to be understood for what it is, interpreted correctly, thoroughly embraced, lived with zeal, and shared in concrete, practical ways.

This Gospel narrative did not just happen when Christ walked the earth some two thousand years ago. It continues to unfold itself in the lives of his followers who seek to have his narrative reflected in their own lives. Because we know we cannot do this by ourselves, we rely on God's help as we walk by faith through this wounded world, live in hope as we journey through life with our eyes steadily focused on our Lord, and seek to love and serve those around us. We do all this, because we understand with the Apostle Paul that we too have been crucified with Christ (Gal 2: 19) and that the unleashing of Christ's Spirit upon the world at Pentecost empowers us live as Christ lived and love as he loved.

Because of Christ's Gospel narrative, his Spirit dwells within our hearts and we dwell in his. Because of this narrative, we have become adopted sons and daughters of the Father. Because of this narrative, we too can enter the worlds of those around us. We too can give ourselves completely to them. We too can become nourishment for them. We too can be a source of hope for them. As the Apostle Paul reminds us, "For all who are led by the Spirit of God are children of God. For you did not receive a spirit of slavery to fall back into fear, but you have received a spirit of adoption. When we cry, 'Abba! Father!' it is that very Spirit bearing witness with our spirit that we are children of God, and if children, then heirs, heirs of God and joint heirs with Christ—if, in fact, we suffer with him so that we may also be glorified with him" (Rom 8:14-

17). The goal of Christ's Gospel narrative is for us to share with him the glory of the Father. As we eagerly await the coming of that day, let us strive to make his narrative intimately one with our own.